Greetings from

NEW·YORK·CITY

Bruce Marshall

THUNDER BAY
P·R·E·S·S

San Diego, California

The Birth of a City

A port where the world and its dreamers were welcome

The southern tip of Manhattan island was the ideal location for the nation's front door, and for its trade entrance with its tranquil moorings. And, once the Erie Canal connected the Great Lakes with the Hudson River, it became a waterway into the heart of the continent.

Lower Manhattan burgeoned with all the raw disorder of a haphazard development: a confusion of nationalities as mariners jumped ship, and a labyrinth of streets and lanes contained to the north by the rampart that would become Wall Street. But in 1811 there appeared an ordered vision for the island's future—a grid plan of broad north-south avenues and cross streets at 200-feet intervals, with only the old native trail of Broadway left to meander diagonally among the city blocks.

Woodlands were hacked down, the landscape flattened, stubborn hillocks shoveled into unstable swamps. Soon, investors like John Jacob Astor—who had made his first fortune by importing a shipload of Chinese porcelain, silk, and spices—were buying city blocks ever

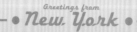

more distantly northward, selling them to developers for huge profit, and celebrating by building their own grand mansions along Fifth Avenue.

By 1900 most of the 2,000 city blocks ordained by the grid plan were developed—though, at this time, mostly by four-story buildings. The population reached 1 million, and continued to climb, accommodating most of the nation's millionaires and harboring bottom-feeding migrants in the dense slums of the original port area.

And with skyscraper-building now a possibility, with the city incorporating the potential of five boroughs—Manhattan, Brooklyn, the Bronx, Queens, and Staten Island—New York was ready to reach for the sky and fulfill its dreams.

Above: An 18th-century map. Materials for building New York came down the East River from Connecticut. The Hudson led to the riches of the backcountry.

Right: Classic New York's picture postcards celebrate its bright lights, bustling streets, and tall buildings. One futuristic vision was wrong, however: the sky never quite filled with airplanes.

PLAN of the CITY of NEW YORK

WORLD'S FAIR 1964 1965

VIEW FROM BROOKLYN

HOBBLE SKIRT CARS,
ON BROADWAY,
NEW YORK CITY.

5

Statue of Liberty

Carrying the torch for New York

Bits and pieces of the Statue of Liberty were put on a teasing display in Paris, then in Philadelphia and New York, in eager fund-raising campaigns. Public subscription in France paid for the construction of this gift from the French nation, a work by the sculptor Frédéric-Auguste Bartholdi; all that was required of Americans was to pay for its granite-and-concrete pedestal on Bedloe's Island. This took an embarrassingly long

Above: The torch topping the 150-foot-high statue, which sits on a 140-foot-high base.

Below: Toes and torch: the pieces were shipped from France in packing cases, to be assembled on site.

time—twenty years—but finally the newspaper publisher Joseph Pulitzer bullied readers of the world into making enough nickel and dime contributions. President Grover Cleveland dedicated "Lady Liberty" on October 28, 1886. During her first thirty years in place, she would be the first sight of America for 20 million immigrants.

Above: Bartholdi (bottom right) explains the internal iron construction to a top-hatted visitor. Gustave Eiffel, builder of the Eiffel Tower, advised on the structuring necessary to cope with the harbor's gales.

Ellis Island

Landfall for the world's weary

The first waves of immigrants landed directly on the island of Manhattan, at Battery Park. But as the numbers arriving grew—they would become a million a year in the early 1900s—a dedicated housing facility was required, one that caused less disturbance to the residents.

Above: At Battery Park, handcarts met new arrivals. Their first stopping point was usually among their own homeland communities in the ghettoes of Lower Manhattan.

Ellis Island, just off the New Jersey shore—three acres with a checkered history as the site of gallows for hanging pirates and as an ammunition dump—was chosen. The first

Above: An old lantern slide depicts disembarkation, carefully placing the Statue of Liberty in the background.

complex of wooden buildings, destroyed by fire, was replaced in brick and concrete at the turn of the century.

New arrivals could be comforted in dormitories and schoolrooms, but faced the ordeal of interviews and tests in hearings rooms and quarantine wards. Inspectors could deny entry for any one of some sixty reasons, usually medical, but sometimes polygamy and pauperism. And officials impatient with long, unspellable foreign names, might send successful arrivals on their way with new identities, like Mr. and Mrs. Sunshine.

Above: Immigrants enjoy their first taste of American food in the dining hall at Ellis Island.

Curiously and undemocratically, hopefuls who could afford to arrive as first- and second-class passengers on regular, scheduled voyages were not processed in this way: they were waved through casual controls at the Hudson River port.

Above: Over the years, Ellis Island grew tenfold, to almost 30 acres. The facility closed in 1954, though the principal buildings have been restored as a museum of immigration.

Empire State Building

New York's own "wonder of the world"

Skyscraper folklore has it that men of a particular Native American tribe were the construction heroes—fearless at heights, and nonchalantly riveting, welding, and munching lunch perched on nine-inch-wide crossbeams high above the street. In fact, there's truth to it: they were members of the Mohawk tribe, whose head for heights had first been noticed when they were recruited in their Montreal homeland for the Canadian Pacific Railroad's bridge-building program.

When it came to building the Empire State Building, unemployed victims of the Great Depression's lay-offs and shutdowns, eager for work, hid their fears and joined them on a project whose architect was briefed "build a structure as tall as you can that won't fall over."

The most dramatic performers were the four-man riveting teams whose daily work, come rain, wind, or shine, was a precision high-wire

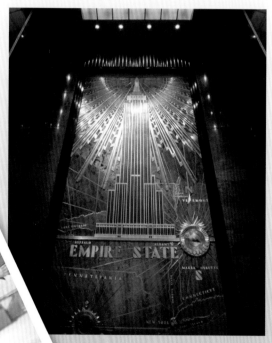

Above: A portfolio by the photographer Lewis W. Hine paid tribute to the intrepid construction workers. No hard hats or safety harnesses at this address!

Above: The three-story-high lobby features an aluminum relief depicting the building.

Left: There are 6,500 windows to wash (left), 1,860 steps to sweep, and more than 70 elevators for daily dusting.

Right: The vision for the building was that transatlantic airships would disembark to rooftop gangplanks. However, tests with blimps indicated that the visionaries hadn't allowed for the winds at that height.

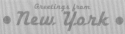

Right: In the 1933 movie *King Kong*, a giant ape seeks to evade capture by climbing the building, but falls to his death. The Empire State Building's most dramatic real-life incident came when a B-52 military airplane crashed into it on a foggy day in 1945.

act that connected the skeleton's beams of Pittsburgh steel with red-hot slugs of iron.

The Empire State's frame arose at a rate of a floor a day until in 1931, just a year and six weeks after ground-breaking, New Yorkers could see that their beloved Fifth Avenue was home to the world's tallest building, a title it

would lose to the World Trade Center forty-one years later. By 2010, however, it was down at fourteenth place, outstripped by the world's tallest, Burj Khalifa in Dubai.

Left and right: Getting close (left), and then completed (right). The broadcast tower was added in 1953, giving the building a full height of 1,453 feet.

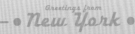

Chrysler Building

Highlight of the golden age of skyscrapers

Above: 405 Lexington Avenue—one of the entrances to the Chrysler Building, with the triangular hubcap motif strongly present. In the lobby behind, elaborate murals celebrate productivity and quality workmanship.

Walter P. Chrysler, who launched America's first aerodynamic, streamlined car, the Chrysler Airflow, commissioned the most flamboyant landmark of the time. To one contemporary critic, the Chrysler Building was "an oversize jukebox;" but many would argue that it is still the world's most beautiful skyscraper where Art Deco meets the Jazz Age in a radiant riot of angles and curves.

Chrysler paid the bills with his own money, not the corporation's, for the building was to be his children's inheritance. Then the budget had to stretch as he got caught up in "height wars," the rivalry to create the world's tallest

building. The other contender at the time was 40 Wall Street (now the Trump Building), being built by a partner of Chrysler's architect, William Van Alen.

When it seemed that Chrysler's tower would lose out by just a few feet, Van Alen commissioned a stainless steel spire, 185 feet tall, that was furtively brought into the building in sections. In one dramatic 90-minute shift in November, 1929, the spire pierced the top of the building to be riveted in place, topping out at 1,047 feet. The "tallest

Above and left: Gleaming ribs and triangular windows set in the dome's curves. At corner setbacks, Chrysler hood ornaments inspire the wings to ceremonial urns.

building" status lasted just eleven months—until the Empire State Building took the title. But the Chrysler Building remains New Yorkers' favorite, a dazzling display of Art Deco that gets more beautiful the higher it gets.

Below: The top of the tower is the best part—diminishing tiers of stainless steel in tightening curves.

Flatiron Building

A new angle on office building

Fifth Avenue at Twenty-third Street was a prime piece of real estate ripe for development at the turn of the twentieth century. The problem was that this was where undisciplined Broadway meandered across the center avenue of the city's grid plan, leaving an untidy triangular plot.

Architect Daniel Burnham was not deterred. A pioneer of the Chicago School of architecture that was leading the nation's experiments with tall buildings, he sketched a bravura concept for an office block. The building

Above: A nod to classicism—decorative pillars supporting the cornice.

duly took shape: a steel skeleton offering a shiplike prow, limestone facades at the lower levels, and glazed terra-cotta above. Proportions and decoration in Italian Renaissance style, complemented the confident Beaux-Arts flourishes.

New Yorkers were convinced that Burnham's Folly—twenty-two floors, 285 feet high—would blow over in the wind. In the event, the swirling winds had the most dramatic effect at ground level—as downdrafts lifted the skirts and petticoats of the elegant shoppers on Ladies' Mile.

The "ship" still sails up the avenue, still a spectacular subject for tourists' cameras, and executives still vie for a front corner office.

Left: The Flatiron Building was properly the Fuller Building, named for its first owners. It marked the end of Ladies' Mile, where the new notions of window shopping and retail therapy were promoted by glamorous storefronts and the first department stores, including R.H. Macy.

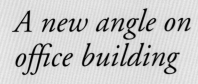

New York in Film

Prime billing for the location

John D. Rockefeller had set his heart on building an opera house as the centerpiece of the Rockefeller Center, his visionary project in Midtown Manhattan. But it was the time

Above and right: In *Ghostbusters* (1984) a "paranormal exterminator service," operating out of an abandoned firestation in TriBeCa, apply their talents in a Central Park West apartment.

of the Great Depression. The supporters he needed withdrew. So Rockefeller decided to serve less elitist tastes; the result was Radio City Music Hall. If any building in the city could be called a people's palace, this was it.

Impatient New Yorkers were prepared to wait in lines around the block to be among audiences of 6,000 for star performers backed

Above: "Jets" taunt "Sharks" in *West Side Story* (1961). The movie was shot at San Juan Hill, a Puerto Rican ghetto that made way for the Lincoln Center for the Performing Arts.

Left: Radio City Music Hall is nicknamed "the Showplace of the Nation".

Right: Spider-Man found ingenious ways of getting around the city in the movie of that name (2002) and its sequels.

Left: Audrey Hepburn ogles the jewelry store in *Breakfast at Tiffany's* (1961) an all-time favorite New York movie.

Below: The exhibits come to life at the American Museum of Natural History in *Night at the Museum* (2006).

Above: There's a giant piano keyboard on the floor of the FAO Schwarz toy store on Fifth Avenue. Tom Hanks danced on it in *Big* (1988).

by a sixty-piece pit orchestra and the Rockettes—the resident, world-famous dance company. But there would also be a movie in Radio City shows, and this was a movie house without peer: a golden curtain arose to reveal the world's largest cinema screen, and a giant Wurlitzer theater organ, rising on a shimmering platform, accompanied the movie's opening credits.

Radio City was far from being the first movie theater, but its grandeur and glamor turned New Yorkers into movie addicts. As a result, they eagerly promoted their city as a movie set. It has become the most used of all urban locations.

Below: The familiar features of a classic New York diner in *When Harry Met Sally* (1989).

13

The City that Never Sleeps

Nights of a thousand stars

Broadway is the city's bustling backbone, but the name has also come to mean the grand concept of show business—

representing the city's devotion to the lively arts. New York's first theaters were, indeed, on lower Broadway, the boulevard; but Broadway as a concept spread wider than that, to colonize Times Square (where the composer Oscar Hammerstein built three theaters), to take over Forty-

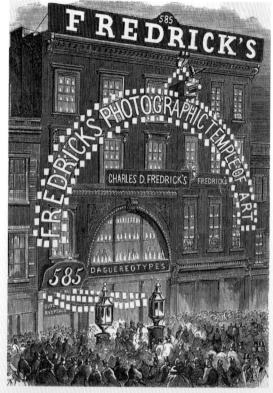

Above: Banjo-playing minstrels were the performers at Perham's Opera House on Broadway.

Left and below: More recently at Broadway addresses: a revival of *West Side Story* at the Palace, and David Letterman's *Late Show*, televised at what was the Ed Sullivan Theater.

Above: A 60-foot curve of lamps advertized C.D. Fredrick's photographic studio and attracted the crowds.

Below: A discreet sign over the door identifies one of the city's favorite jazz clubs, in Greenwich Village.

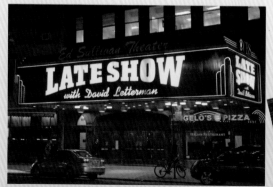

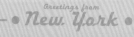

Right: The 1987 New York opening of *Les Misérables* was at the Broadway Theater, on Broadway.

Below: The Apollo Theater, long a central feature of musical life in Harlem, hosted a Michael Jackson tribute in 2010.

second Street and settle on more northerly streets straddling Sixth and Seventh Avenues.

There's another address that became a related concept, and this one doesn't exist as a street at all. That's Tin Pan Alley, named for the tinny sound of audition pianos in the poky rooms where composers introduced musical scores, and potential stars, to impresarios. And there's another name for the Broadway concept—the Great White Way. Show business is an after-dark pleasure; maximum wattage, as colorful and as lively as possible, flashes a welcome greeting—and nowhere is it done better than on Broadway.

Right: The stars come out on Broadway (right, from top): Elvis Presley rehearses for the *Ed Sullivan Show* in 1957. Gwen Verdon and Jerry Orbach in the original production of *Chicago* (1975). Richard Burton as Hamlet; the play directed as a "dress rehearsal" in 1964 by John Gielgud.

Take Me out to the Ballgame

Mets and Yankees

While other baseball franchises have fled to the west coast, the Mets and the Yankees continue to fly their pennants for New York—the Mets in Queens, the Yankees in the Bronx. Indeed, the Mets were founded in response to those 1950s departures, to maintain a National League presence in the area, and their uniforms adapted the Dodgers' colors of blue and white and the Giants', orange and black.

After early camping-out, the Mets made their home at Shea Stadium, on the old World's Fair site at Flushing Meadows—an arena notorious for its noisy position under the flight path into La Guardia. Their new stadium, the $850-million Citi Field,

Left: Mr. Mets was the first "live" Major League mascot.

built alongside, hosted its first regular season game in April 2009.

The Yankees also have a new home—a second Yankee Stadium, across the street from the old one. It made news for its cost, estimated to be more than $2 billion; for the high price of the best seats, said to be among the highest in professional sport; and for the enormous tally of home runs in its first season, 2009. In this slightly smaller park, there were 237

Above and left: The Mets' Citi Field scoreboard announces the club's newest acquisition, Jason Bay (in April 2010). Mike Piazza (left) is a longer-serving hero. He was the best-hitting catcher of all time, with 427 home runs to his credit.

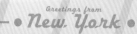

Sporting heroes, proud moments

home runs, bringing back into circulation the old nickname for the Yankees—the Bronx Bombers, coined for the hitting power of players from Babe Ruth onward.

Above: Yankees pitcher Don Larsen pitched the first perfect World Series game—one of only 20 perfect games in MLB history—against the against the Brooklyn Dodgers on October 8, 1956.

Above right: Babe Ruth wears his crown as the "King of Swat." He hit a home run in the first game at Yankee Stadium—"the house that Ruth built"—in 1923.

Below right: Derek Jeter was a later star, the Yankees' captain and winner of both Most Valuable Player and Sportsman of the Year awards.

Baseball's Lost Shrines

The sport feels the city's pressures

Ebbets Field is a more appealing place in Brooklyn's memory than it was in real life, especially in the cramped and decaying form of its final days. But the name has come to symbolize a lost golden age of baseball as the home of the Brooklyn Dodgers and their truly devoted army of fans.

The problem became that as the team prospered, so did the fans, and they tended to move ever farther from the park, out into the Long Island suburbs. There could never be enough parking spaces for them on game days in Flatbush, Brooklyn, so the club's owner Walter O'Malley planned a new stadium on a freshly cleared Brooklyn site.

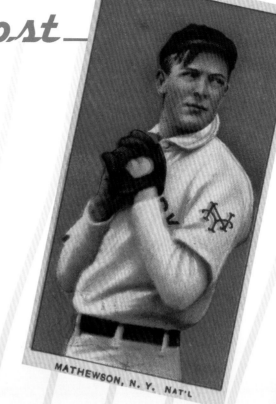

Above: Christy Mathewson, a pre–World War I Giants' pitcher, was one of the "First Five" inductees into the National Baseball Hall of Fame and Museum.

Parks Commissioner Robert Moses wanted any new facility to be built in Flushing Meadows, Queens. O'Malley threatened to move the Dodgers to Los Angeles. Moses stood firm. So did O'Malley. The "most infamous abandonment" in sport came after the 1957 season.

To be followed—at O'Malley's vengeful urging, some say—by the Dodgers' cross-town rivals, the Giants, who vacated the Polo Grounds to settle in San Francisco. The Polo

Grounds they left was the fourth stadium with that name in northern Manhattan. The first was, indeed, a polo field, at 110th Street. A professional baseball team began playing there in 1880. The Giants won five World Series when Polo Grounds IV was their home.

There is still major league baseball in the city, at the new incarnation of Yankee Stadium and at Citi Field, which has replaced Shea as the Mets' home.

Above: A Dodger slides safely home at Ebbets Field. The catcher is the Yankees' Yogi Berra.

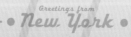

Polo Grounds, New York City,
Home of the New York Giants.

ALL BROOKLYN HONORS THE Dodgers
1947 NATIONAL LEAGUE CHAMPS

Clockwise from above: the Polo Grounds, Ebbets
Field, Yankee Stadium, Shea Stadium—homes of the Giants,
Dodgers, Yankees, Mets.

19

A Team for Every Season

Giants and Jets lead the way

The Polo Grounds and Shea Stadium—sport battlegrounds within the city limits that stir proud memories for older New York football fans. But now there are more rewarding uses for prime city real estate than as stadia and parking lots for a short season of football.

So it's now an expedition to New Jersey to support the Giants and the Jets, the teams representing "the New York metropolitan area." That woolly identity and the location beyond the Hudson provoke a loyalty crisis for some. Mayor Ed Koch refused the Giants a Super Bowl city ceremony, calling them "foreigners." However, Mayor Michael Bloomberg authorized a ticker-tape parade in honor of their victory in Super Bowl XLII.

The teams share a stadium, Meadowlands, in East Rutherford, in among a sports complex that includes a race track and an indoor arena. Both teams have bitter personal rivals in the NFL, but they're not, as used to be, each other. And the stadium

Above: Quarterback Eli Manning flaunts the Vince Lombardi Trophy after the underdog Giants beat the favored New England Patriots 17–14 in Superbowl XLII. "The greatest victory in the history of this franchise," said the co-owner.

Right: The Jets' defense at work.

is ingeniously prepared for its double life—a change of identity can be evidenced within just a few hours: the endzone turf is changed to display the right team's symbols, ingenious lighting switches the color of the arena's skin of aluminum louvers—blue for the Giants, green for the Jets.

Neither team has been unrelentingly successful. The Giants are the senior partners, having joined the National Football League in 1925; the Jets were founded in 1959. For a nostalgic draft of that warm winning feeling, the Jets' older fans recall the 1965–68 years, the glorious era when coach Weeb Ewbank and quarterback Joe Namath

carried off Super Bowl III. Football may have left town, but winter's other major pro sports, hockey and basketball, flourish in the heart of Manhattan, both at the favorite entertainment venue, Madison Square Garden.

The Rangers have played hockey here (although "here" has been two different buildings, the present one being a 1960s construction) since their formation in 1926 as the Garden's resident team. They finished their first season with the best record in the NHL. The next year they won the Stanley Cup. New York fans quickly took to "the classiest team in hockey," and by World War II, Rangers' games at the Garden had become glamorous events

Above: The Islanders, too, are a New York team, but play out of Uniondale, Long Island. Here, center Nate Thompson (blue uniform) tangles with the Montreal Canadiens' defense in a 2009 game. In the 1980s, The Islanders won the Stanley Cup four seasons in a row.

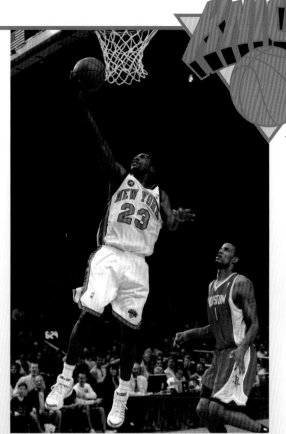

Above: The Knicks' Toney Douglas goes for the basket against the Houston Rockets.

Right: Ukrainian-born Russian international Nikolai Zherdev (top) had a brief stay at the Garden with the Rangers.

attracting show biz, sporting celebrities, and high society.

October to April is the season for both hockey and basketball, and it's the Knicks who represent the city on court, as they've done since 1946. They've been championship winners twice, and Conference title holders

eight times. Wilt Chamberlain once scored 100 points against them, an NBA record; in the 2009–10 season, they suffered the worst home loss in Garden history—by 50 points against the Dallas Mavericks. Then, later in the season, after a team shake-up, they beat the Mavericks 128–94.

Only in New York

When the streets come alive for a party

As befits a show biz capital, New York elevates its citizens' ceremonies into spectacular blazes of light, color, and noise. Not just a shamrock buttonhole for St. Patrick's Day, but the world's largest, loudest Irish parade; not just a witch's hat and a pumpkin at Halloween, but 50,000

Clockwise from above: The New Year's Eve ball descends the flagpole at One Times Square. "Everyone is Irish" for the St. Patrick's Day parade. Helium-filled balloons are the stars of Macy's Thanksgiving Day parade. A ticker tape welcome for Charles Lindbergh in 1927.

Right: Not so much a party, but certainly a community outing, runners in the New York Marathon cross the Verrazano-Narrows Bridge.

costumes and 2 million spectators in Greenwich Village; not just a hero's handshake on the steps of City Hall, but a storm of shredded paper raining on a procession.

This last, ticker tape processions, are less frequent than they once were—a guilty conscience about waste and recycling, maybe— but New York finds many excuses for a party.

And the world joins in. It's estimated that 2 billion television viewers mime the countdown as that 12-foot ball of light welcomes the New Year to Times Square.

Above and below: The Christmas tree at Rockefeller Center is usually about 90 feet tall and decorated with as many as 30,000 lights. Fireworks and a "golden mile" of sparklers over the East River (below) were a Fourth of July tradition, but the party has now moved to the Hudson.

Brooklyn Bridge

Building "the eighth wonder of the world"

Above: John A. Roebling studied bridge-building as an engineering student in Berlin. One of his first American ventures was the suspension bridge at Niagara Falls.

Above: Fireworks on opening night. Then the bridge would be electrically lit by Thomas Edison's new power station.

By the 1850s, Brooklyn was the third-largest city in the United States, its destiny inevitably linked with Manhattan's. The East River ferries between the cities carried 100,000 passengers a day, and it was on one such uncomfortable journey, blocked by winter ice flows, that John A. Roebling resolved to bridge this, the world's busiest waterway.

Roebling was indeed a bridge builder, but his other interest was manufacturing steel wire and cable, and this was the key to his faith that a single span of 1,600 feet—twice the distance so far achieved—was possible, and that it could be 130 feet above mean high water, to allow passage of the tall ships of the time.

It took Roebling ten years to convince city fathers and financiers that the plan was feasible, and another fourteen years for it to be accomplished—at twice the original budget. Roebling died as the project got under way. His son, Washington Roebling, took over, and was soon to experience the strange, debilitating condition that was invaliding the workers whose task was installing foundations well below the waterline: this was caisson disease, decompression sickness—"the bends."

But on May 24, 1893, one of the century's great engineering achievements, the "eighth wonder of the world," opened, and proud locals enjoyed the views from the highest man-made promenade yet built.

Above: Job interviews were conducted on this temporary footpath, to check that recruits had a head for heights.

Above: A cable has spanned the East River. Master mechanic E. Frank Farrington makes the much-publicized first crossing.

Getting Around

To work and to play, the train takes the strain

Tunneling through the city's stone base to create a subway system was too daunting a challenge in the mid-nineteenth century, so New York tried a railroad network on stilts—the eccentric El (for "elevated") that brought noisome gloom to major Manhattan avenues for over half a century.

However, when the five boroughs came together as Greater New York, it was obvious

Above: An early crossing of the skeletal Brooklyn Bridge.

Left: The big, boxy Checker cab was the best-known wearer of the famous yellow livery.

Above: Converging on the Holland Tunnel. By the 1930s, 12 million vehicles a year were using it—paying a 50-cent toll.

that the El was not fit for the spreading city's purposes. And once borers got burrowing, there was no holding back the subway: 16 miles of underground track in four early years. Today, 250 miles of routes, amounting to almost 1,000 miles of track underground and overground, provide the world's most extensive rapid transit system.

Most Americans drive to work—but not New Yorkers; their households are way below the national average for car ownership. They take well over 5 million subway rides each weekday. And 2 million bus rides. Or they hail one of the city's 13,000 yellow cabs. Staten

Above: That New Yorkers are committed to public transport might not have been obvious to drivers caught up in this Seventh Street rush hour.

Subway

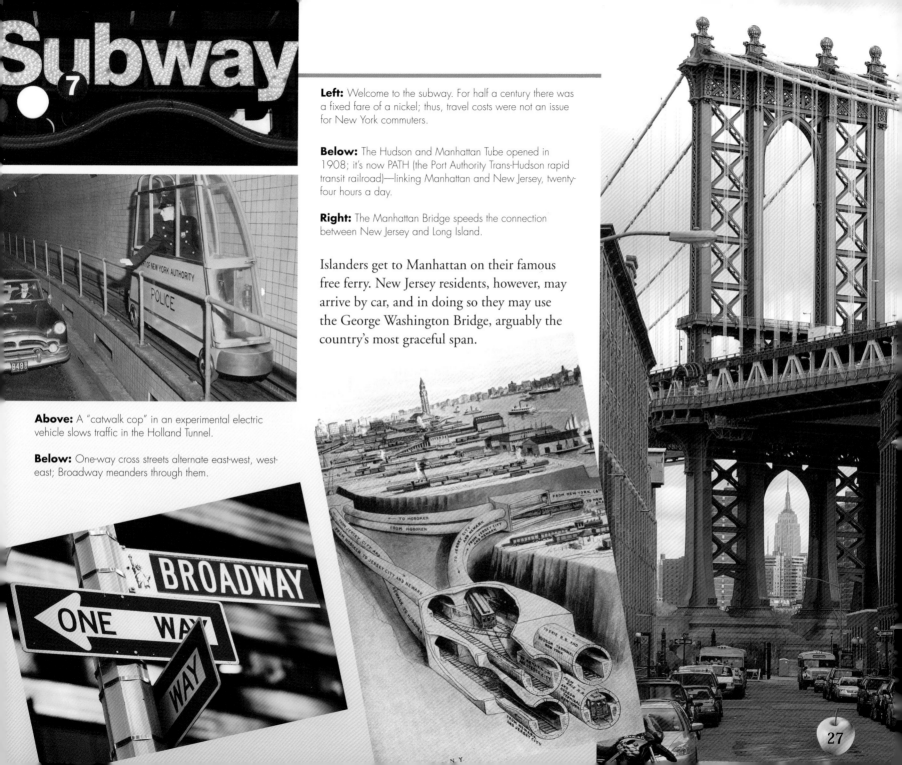

Left: Welcome to the subway. For half a century there was a fixed fare of a nickel; thus, travel costs were not an issue for New York commuters.

Below: The Hudson and Manhattan Tube opened in 1908; it's now PATH (the Port Authority Trans-Hudson rapid transit railroad)—linking Manhattan and New Jersey, twenty-four hours a day.

Right: The Manhattan Bridge speeds the connection between New Jersey and Long Island.

Islanders get to Manhattan on their famous free ferry. New Jersey residents, however, may arrive by car, and in doing so they may use the George Washington Bridge, arguably the country's most graceful span.

Above: A "catwalk cop" in an experimental electric vehicle slows traffic in the Holland Tunnel.

Below: One-way cross streets alternate east-west, west-east; Broadway meanders through them.

Central Park

The green heart of a crowded city

As the city blocks marked on the grid plan filled with buildings, as the development relentlessly moved northward, leisure areas became an issue. The waterfronts, east and west, might have provided it—nowhere on Manhattan

Above: Frederick Law Olmsted. At first, streetcar fares from the tenements put his park out of reach of the city's poor.

island was more than a mile from a river—but there the gloomy trappings of docks and transport were taking over.

Way north of the growing city was a tract of land, 800-odd acres, whose marshlands and rock outcrops gave pause to the property developers. Landscapers moved in, settlers, squatters and pig farmers were moved out, some at gunpoint, and Central Park took shape. The landscapers were Frederick Law Olmsted and

Above left: Promoting a bullfight in the park. It was not to the death, however: "matadors" with capes teased Texas steers borrowed from the stockyard.

Left: Another imported European pleasure as gondolas cruise the boating lake.

Above: Overlooking the naturalistic landscape of the Lake is one of the park's most formal features, Bethesda Terrace.

Calvert Vaux, whose vision of a seamless patch of countryside in the city was acknowledged as "nineteenth-century America's greatest work of art."

Above: A sensationalist cartoon plays on a 19th-century scare that Central Park Lake emitted poisonous vapors.

Right: Central Park in the fall.

Below: The commissioners' report for 1869 contained this suggestion for employing the menagerie.

Reaching for the Sky

The rise of a great city

That first view of Manhattan—whether it's from an approaching ship, or from an airplane swooping into La Guardia, or looking up from the traffic on the Triborough Bridge—is perhaps the most dramatic of all cityscapes. Much of that skyline is a pageant of corporate posturing.

For what could be better than a skyscraper as evidence of influence and prestige, preferably with the company logo displayed a few stories higher than those of rivals?

Downtown, Wall Street is at the heart of it, with the financial houses enabled by modern communications to be world players. Midtown

Above: Once the dominant architectural structure, the Brooklyn Bridge is now visually overwhelmed by the towers of Manhattan.

Left: Steaming past her home backdrop, The *SS United States* makes her stately way to Pier 86, before earning the Blue Riband for the fastest Atlantic crossing in 1952.

is a required address for those businesses whose global ambitions are helped by proximity to the United Nations headquarters, and Midtown Madison Avenue is the hub of the nation's marketing activity.

There had to some planning laws, however, or the city would have filled with straight-

sided blocks whose only virtue was height. Early rules required setbacks as a building rose, allowing sunlight to reach the street. More recently, straight-sided buildings have been acceptable, but their developers have had to provide public space around them—the "plaza bonus."

Thus, that famous skyline does have character toppings and a plethora of shapes. And in among it all, hidden away, there are still some of the brownstone townhouses and four-story apartment blocks of a more neighborly era.

Left, above, and right: The Twin Towers of the World Trade Center (left) lost the title "world's tallest" to Chicago's Sears Tower in 1974. Two vertical columns of light at Ground Zero (above) mark the anniversary of the 9/11 attacks. The spire of the Freedom Tower (right, center) which is replacing the doomed buildings, is to top out at 1,776 feet.

Wish You Were Here

All the ways of sending greetings

From Paris, the picture postcard mailed home is likely to feature twelfth-century Notre Dame; from Rome it would be the Colosseum, as ancient as the city itself. No such relics to photograph in New York, however. There's nothing much to show from before those proud symbols of mid-nineteenth century energy and engineering, the Statue of Liberty and the Brooklyn Bridge.

So, when mass vacationing took hold between the world wars, the greetings sent home by New York's growing hordes of visitors

Above: Manhattan's defining skyline starts to take shape: as tall spires begin to punctuate the horizon.

depicted images as down-to-earth as the citizens themselves: tollbooths and traffic jams, subway maps, and billboards.

Above: Worth writing home about: the parkways were for autos only; trucks and buses were banned.

Above: A tranquil beach setting at Coney Island. The truth was a million visitors a day, and more hot dogs than lobsters.

Above: Big, bold outlines for the city's treats and treasures.

Left: Times Square in the 1940s, and Fifth Avenue around 1910. Heavy traffic was a problem even then.

Greetings from New York City

POST CARD

PLACE
STAMP
HERE

Greetings from Manhattan, New York City

POST CARD

PLACE
STAMP
HERE

Brooklyn Bridge and Manhattan Bridge

POST CARD

PLACE
STAMP
HERE

New York 1849, looking south from Union Square

POST CARD

PLACE
STAMP
HERE